I0878782

UNBELIEVABLE!

# 34 AMAZING FACTS ABOUT SOCCER

Hannah Gramson

Lerner Publications ◆ Minneapolis

Copyright © 2026 by Lerner Publishing Group, Inc.

Stats in this book are accurate through April 1, 2025.

All rights reserved. International copyright secured. No part of this book may be reproduced, stored in a retrieval system, or transmitted in any form or by any means—electronic, mechanical, photocopying, recording, or otherwise—without the prior written permission of Lerner Publishing Group, Inc., except for the inclusion of brief quotations in an acknowledged review.

Lerner Publications Company
An imprint of Lerner Publishing Group, Inc.
241 First Avenue North
Minneapolis, MN 55401 USA

For reading levels and more information, look up this title at www.lernerbooks.com.

Main body text set in ITC Franklin Gothic Std.
Typeface provided by Adobe Systems.

**Editor:** Elena Mai **Designer:** Mary Ross
**Lerner team:** Sue Marquis

**Library of Congress Cataloging-in-Publication Data**

Names: Gramson, Hannah author
Title: 34 amazing facts about soccer / Hannah Gramson.
Other titles: Thirty-four amazing facts about soccer
Description: Minneapolis : Lerner Publications, 2026. | Series: UpDog books. Unbelievable | Includes bibliographical references and index. | Audience: Ages 8–11 | Audience: Grades 2–3 | Summary: "Billions of fans worldwide tune into soccer's World Cup every year, making soccer the world's most popular sport. Explore the sport's history, awesome goals, superstar players, and more in this exciting collection of fun facts"— Provided by publisher.
Identifiers: LCCN 2025011514 | ISBN 9798765689769 library binding | ISBN 9798348029524 paperback | ISBN 9798765699706 epub
Subjects: LCSH: Soccer—History—Juvenile literature
Classification: LCC GV943.25 .G727 2026 | DDC 796.334—dc23/eng/20250414

LC record available at https://lccn.loc.gov/2025011514

Manufactured in the United States of America
1-1012515-54844-7/1/2025

# Table of Contents

# THE WORLD'S SPORT

Cuju was one of the earliest forms of soccer. It was played in China over two thousand years ago.

Players scored by kicking a leather ball through a goal on a raised net.

Modern soccer began in England in the 1800s.

The first international game took place in 1872.

The game was between Scotland and England. The final score was 0–0.

The first known women's soccer game was in 1895.

Up Next!

**ALL-TIME GREATS.**

# BREAKING RECORDS

In 2012, striker Lionel Messi played for Barcelona and Argentina. He scored 91 total goals.

No other player has scored so many goals in one year.

In 2021, British goalkeeper Tom King scored a goal from 105 yards (96 m) away.

It's the longest goal ever scored.

In 2022, Canada's Christine Sinclair scored her 190th career international goal.

She holds the record for the most international goals scored.

# LIST BREAK!

Who has scored the most goals in international soccer? Here are the top five highest-scoring players in men's international soccer.

1. Cristiano Ronaldo, Portugal (136)
2. Lionel Messi, Argentina (112)
3. Ali Daei, Iran (108)
4. Sunil Chhetri, India (95)
5. Mokhtar Dahari, Malaysia (89)

Cristiano Ronaldo

Abby Wambach

Here are the top five highest-scoring players in women's international soccer.

1. Christine Sinclair, Canada (190)
2. Abby Wambach, USA (184)
3. Mia Hamm, USA (158)
4. Maysa Jbarah, Jordan (137)
5. Carli Lloyd, USA (134)

Up Next!

## WORLD COMPETITION.

# WORLD CUP

The first Men's World Cup was held in 1930.

Brazil has won the most Men's World Cups. It has won five times.

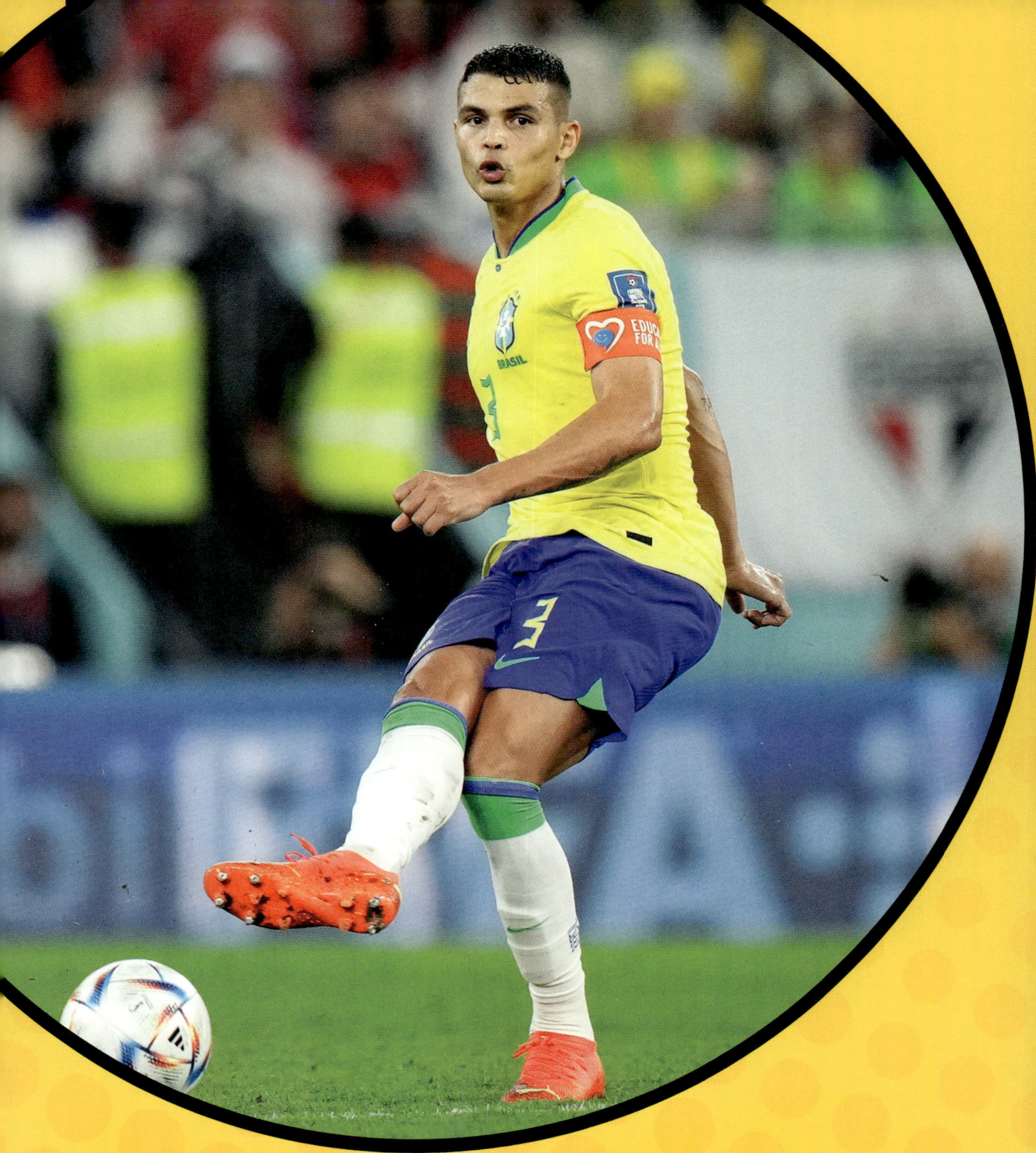

It's also the only country to have played in every Men's World Cup.

The first Women's World Cup took place in 1991.

The US beat Norway 2–1 in the final.

The US has the most Women's World Cup wins. It has won four times.

## Up Next!

**on TV.**

# AMAZING BUT TRUE

The first international game on TV was in 1938.

Scotland beat England 1–0.

Soccer balls were all brown or white before 1970.

Black was added to make the ball easier to see on TV.

In 2022, 1.5 billion people watched the Men's World Cup final. Argentina beat France in penalty kicks.

It was the most watched soccer game of all time. Which soccer team is your favorite?

## Glossary

**international:** involving two or more countries

**leather:** a material made from animal skin

**modern:** the present or recent past

**penalty kick:** a free kick at the goal allowed for certain fouls or to decide the winner of some games

**striker:** a player whose main job is to score goals

**World Cup:** an international soccer competition played every four years

## Check It Out!

Britannica Kids: Soccer
https://kids.britannica.com/kids/article/soccer/353786

Goldstein, Margaret J. *Women's Professional Soccer.* Lerner Publications, 2026.

Golkar, Golriz. *Cristiano Ronaldo*. Bellwether Media, 2024.

Rajczak Nelson, Kristen. *Mia Hamm: Soccer GOAT*. Gareth Stevens, 2024.

US Women's National Soccer Team
https://www.ussoccer.com/teams/uswnt

US Youth Soccer
https://www.usyouthsoccer.org

# Index



# Photo Acknowledgments

Image credits: CPA Media Pte Ltd/Alamy, p. 4; View Stock/Alamy, p. 5; powerofforever/Getty Images, p. 6; duncan1890/Getty Images, pp. 7–8; steeve-x-art/Alamy, p. 9; Carlos M. Saavedra/Sports Illustrated via Getty Images, p. 10; AP Photo/Natacha Pisarenko, p. 11; Eddie Garvey/MI News/NurPhoto via AP, p. 12; Press Association via AP Images, p. 13; Darryl Dyck/The Canadian Press via AP, p. 14; AP Photo/Fernando Llano, p. 15; Valter Gouveia/SPP/Sipa USA via AP Images, p. 16; Lars Baron - FIFA via Getty Images, p. 17; AP Photo, p. 18; AP Photo/Luca Bruno, p. 19; Bagu Blanco/Pressinphoto/Sipa USA via AP Images, p. 20; Bob Thomas via Getty Images, p. 21; Sebastian Gollnow/picture-alliance/dpa/AP Images, p. 22; Christian Liewig/Abaca/Sipa USA via AP Images, p. 23; Central Press/Getty Images, p. 24; Douglas Miller/Keystone/Getty Images, p. 25; Dziurek/Getty Images, p. 26; Connect Images/Getty Images, p. 27; Anthony Bibard/FEP/Icon Sport/Sipa USA via AP Images, pp. 28, 29.

Cover: AP Photo/Henrique Casinhas/SOPA Images/Sipa USA.